How to

By Melody Litton

Illustrated by Mana Shoji Riedel

For Brock,
my totally awesome husband

Three years ago I was in my car going nowhere. I pulled to the side of the road and started screaming at the top of my lungs. I was sobbing, pounding on the steering wheel, and shaking uncontrollably. Over and over I repeated "I don't want to do this! I don't want to be married anymore!" After at least 20 minutes of uncontrollable sobbing and screaming I collapsed into the fetal position on the ground beside my car and rocked back and forth in silence.

Three nights ago I laid beside my husband, my legs entwined in his. My head was on his chest listening to his heartbeat and steady breathing. I was overwhelmed with feelings of love. I offered a silent prayer of thanks that this man is mine forever. We then made passionate and beautiful love, real love. It was the kind that unites and empowers, the kind that enlivens your soul, the kind that bonds lovers, both body and spirit, together forever.

As I laid in the dark with my husband, I reflected on that awful night three years prior. Quiet tears spilled from my eyes. How grateful I am that our journey didn't end that day. I could have chosen to walk away. But I didn't. And neither did he.

Our journey continues each day and it will throughout eternity. We still hit potholes on occasion. We still mess up and hurt each other's feelings sometimes. But we're traveling the road together and we're madly in love.

This book contains the secrets to becoming an awesome spouse. The secrets may seem quite simple but they are incredibly powerful. And although I have not mastered them all, I don't want to wait another day before sharing them with the world. Someone may be rocking in desperation on the side of the road right now, needing to know where to turn and unsure how much longer they can go on.

Walking away is not the answer. Awesomeness is. Spouses who choose to become totally awesome enjoy marriages that are beyond the comprehension of most people in this world. Totally awesome marriages do exist. And you can have one. The first step is becoming an awesome spouse. No matter where we are on the road right now, our road can lead to joy and incredible love.

A Totally Awesome Spouse

A Totally Awesome Spouse
Looks in the Mirror

"I evaluate myself with honesty and love. I make desired changes with grace and confidence."

This book isn't for your spouse. It isn't meant to be used to analyze how he or she is doing. It's not designed to give you reason to feel sorry for yourself or to find fault in your companion. This book is meant to help *you* learn the secrets to becoming an awesome spouse. It's about *self*-reflection and *personal* growth.

A totally awesome spouse looks inside. The world teaches us that we are victims of circumstance and products of our environment. We learn when we are young: "It's not *my* fault" and "You *made* me. . ." The strategy of the world is to lay blame and point fingers. But a totally awesome spouse knows that when a finger is pointed, there are three fingers pointing right back.

A totally awesome spouse takes responsibility for the things they have control over and release worry and stress for all things that are beyond their control. They self-reflect regularly to ensure they are staying on track. They monitor their thoughts, language, actions, and attitudes. They devote their time and energy to the things that matter and the things they can control.

This secret is very important and the key to successfully becoming a totally awesome spouse: *You are only in control of yourself*. You are responsible for you and I am responsible for me. Our thoughts, attitudes, behaviors, words, spiritual well-being, physical condition, happiness, and success are inherently and eternally individually owned and governed. No one else owns that responsibility and no one can buy, borrow, or steal that responsibility from any one of us.

We cannot control our spouse and it's not our place to do so. Our purpose and goal must be simple and clear- to learn to take control of ourselves and to become a totally awesome spouse through desire and personal efforts.

A Totally Awesome Spouse
Sets Goals

" I share my hopes and dreams with my companion. We are united as we set goals and create our totally awesome life."

Goals matter. They shape our past, affect our present, and create our future. A person who never consciously sets goals gives away their freedom to create the life they really want. Without goals we float aimlessly and allow a careless wave or wind to determine our direction and have control of what we experience, where we end up, and who we become.

A totally awesome spouse sets goals. They consider where they've been, where they are, and where they desire to be. They take responsibility to create the life they truly want. They visualize dreams, write down goals, and then take steps to achieve them. They set goals designed to bring an abundance of joy and wealth to themselves, to their spouse, and to their family.

This principle is one that took me a long time to understand. I grossly underestimated the power and absolute necessity of having goals. I will never go back to floating aimlessly with the wind now that I have discovered the joy that comes when I wield my power to control the sail.

Goals are most powerful when spoken. In a marriage, it's essential that goals are shared. It's not going to do us any good if we're working toward a future where we live on a sparsely populated island eating only fruit and wild honey while our spouse has set a goal to retire in Manhattan and nightly dine on Filet Mignon. As we share our thoughts and dreams we become more united as lovers and friends.

A totally awesome spouse sets goals large and small. Some goals are designed to affect today and others to affect 50 years down the road. They set goals that invite positive thoughts and energy; never inviting anything negative to sabotage the process. What we focus on becomes our reality.

For instance, a goal of mine used to be: "I want to stop speaking rudely to my husband and criticizing him." That sounds like a pretty decent goal right? Well, I thought it was a good goal. But a totally awesome spouse would recognize right off the bat that it was horrible. The wording of the goal was actually stopping me from achieving my desire. Positive wording vs negative wording makes an incredible difference in whether or not we actually attain our goals. The wording of my goal kept my focus on two things: speaking rudely and criticizing. It was in complete opposition to what I actually wanted to achieve.

A totally awesome spouse would choose wording closer to this: "I rejoice in my husband's strengths. I recognize his efforts and praise him at every opportunity."

Compare the two. Negative wording: "I *want* to stop *speaking rudely* to my husband and *criticizing him*." Positive wording: "I *rejoice* in my husband's strengths. I *recognize his efforts* and *praise him* at every opportunity."

I hope you recognize the profound difference in these two affirmations. One is future tense: "I want to" and the second is present tense: "I rejoice." One uses negative words and the other positive. Goals and the affirmations, or statements, that accompany our goals help us most when in the present tense and when utilizing words that are beautifully positive. At first it may feel strange, perhaps as though we are telling our self a lie. But as we faithfully and enthusiastically repeat these affirmations they help us find the energy and desire to create a better reality, to turn them into truth.

Since you're reading these pages right now I'm hoping that one of your goals is to be a totally awesome spouse. Mine is. Each day I now focus on doing a little more and becoming a little better at being a wife. Throughout this book I will be sharing with you the steps I'm taking and the affirmations I use as I continue this journey. There are those who have set the example and marked the way for us to follow. I am thankful for the example of totally awesome spouses and celebrate that each of us can choose to follow the path they have shown.

A totally awesome spouse sets clear goals. They dream and then design a plan to achieve, keeping the well-being of their companion and joy in their marriage as top priority.

A Totally Awesome Spouse
Gives 100%

"I offer 100% of myself to my companion. Together we find peace, strength, and balance, even when surrounded by a world of chaos."

A typical spouse thinks that a marriage should be 50/50 but a totally awesome spouse knows it takes 100% effort, not 50% to have a successful and happy marriage.

Throughout the past eleven years of my marriage I've noticed a pattern. When I'm struggling, my husband becomes stronger. When he's struggling, I'm given strength. When I go crazy and start throwing things at the wall, he calmly removes the kids from the room and gently instructs me to take a bath. When he comes home super ornery and gripes about everything under the sun, I start looking on the bright side. It's natural to balance one another out and it's how it's meant to be. When we begin to lose that balance is when things go down the drain and emotional chaos begins, feelings are hurt, and love starts to dissipate.

If each partner is willing to give only 50% there will often be a gap between what's being given and what's needed for the marriage to work. There are days and periods of time that a person is incapable of offering his or her fair share. We face illness and accident, emotional stress and mental strain, demands of work, family, schooling, and life in general. Sometimes we are maxed out, unable to offer more than what it takes to merely survive. No matter how "unfair" it seems to be, that's just the way it is. As human beings, sometimes we fall short of what's required of us no matter how hard we try.

In a 50/50 marriage that human limitation will often create a gap between what's needed (100%) and what's being offered. If Brock chose to give 50% but during a period of time I had only 20% to offer, our marriage would have a 30% deficit of what's needed and our relationship would suffer. Now let's consider a marriage where partners are willing to give 100% always. During good times there would be 200% and during hard times it would still stay well above the essential 100%.

Who wouldn't opt for a bank account with plenty of cushion rather than one that constantly rides the line of being overdrawn and often plummets into severe debt?

A totally awesome spouse doesn't try to figure out who's giving what, when, or whether things are "fair". They are always willing to give 100% of themselves, their energy, and their devotion to their spouse and building their marriage. Sometimes one partner carries the weight but there will be other occasions where they will be carried. When we joined hands and hearts in marriage, we decided we were in it for the long haul. It doesn't matter during which part of the road we're pushing, which part we're pulling, and which part we're carried. What *does* matter is that we keep trekking the same road and that we're journeying together, giving all we can the entire way.

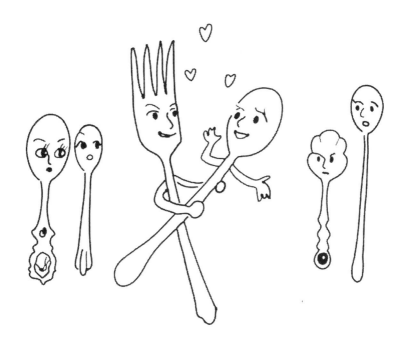

A Totally Awesome Spouse

Chooses to Love

"I choose to love my companion now and forever. Our love grows stronger with each new day."

My husband and I were foster parents for a number of years in Tennessee. We had several children come in and out of our home; two of which we were blessed to be able to adopt. One was a 13 year old with a history of behavioral disorders and the other was a medically fragile infant, born weighing just one and a half pounds and addicted to Methadone. Each of these beautiful girls required a high level of care. Our two biological boys, ages 2 and 3, weren't exactly a piece of cake either.

I quit my full-time job to become a 24/7 full-time mom. Some days I laughed. Some days I sobbed. Other days I hid in the closet and prayed, and prayed, and then prayed some more. But every night as I tucked them in and listened to their prayers or snuck into their room to watch them sleep, I was overcome with feelings of love and gratitude.

Many people have asked me if the love I feel for my adopted children is different than the love I feel for my biological children. The answer in full and complete honesty is no.

We often believe that there's something magical about our blood; being bonded through biological connections. But it's not the biology that matters. It's not the genetic connection that somehow makes us love our children or parents, siblings, cousins, or grandparents. There is an enormous amount of evidence through world history that shows otherwise- mothers throwing babies into trash cans; fathers selling children as slaves; children killing parents; siblings seeking to destroy one another in various ways; members of families abandoning, mistreating, abusing, neglecting, extorting, murdering, and disowning one another.

I love my children, both adopted and biological, because I *choose* to and because I've *devoted* myself to them as their mother. Through my devoted service I've developed a bond with them that is unbreakable, a love that is stronger than anything we will face. When we make the choice to devote ourselves in service to another person, God grants us the amazing blessing of feeling pure love for them. A parent feels this love for their child and a totally awesome spouse feels this love for their companion.

Understanding this reality is vital to becoming a totally awesome spouse. A totally awesome spouse *chooses* to love, even when their companion may be unworthy of that love. A totally awesome spouse *chooses* to serve, even when their companion may be undeserving of that service.

Love is a choice, created and strengthened through giving of ourselves in devoted and willing service. A totally awesome spouse enjoys making the life of their companion better. They find joy in bringing happiness and help to their companion.

I'm not talking about initial attraction, lust, or infatuation. I'm talking about real love; the kind that lasts. The kind of love that holds marriages together forever is created through devoting our attention, thoughts, time, energy, and efforts into keeping the flame burning.

A totally awesome spouse chooses to love their companion and makes that choice their final answer. They continue strengthening that love by devoting themselves 100% to their companion throughout their lives.

Melody Litton

A Totally Awesome Spouse
Makes Time for Play

"I thoroughly enjoy recreational time with my companion. I schedule opportunities for laughter and play, free from distraction and demands."

It's time to take a trip down memory lane. Stop reading and sit back for a few minutes to think about life with your spouse before he/she was your spouse. Remember when you met and the weeks, months, or years of dating before you dived in and tied the knot.

When Brock and I first met we were working in Alaska at a lodge in the middle of nowhere. On our off days we would explore, hike, camp, and splash around in waterfalls. We'd helicopter over mountains and raft around beautiful lakes. We'd hang out in the cafeteria at our work, throw French fries at one another, and practice unwrapping Starbursts with our tongue. When we felt like leaving the wilderness and driving two hours to the nearest town he'd take me to movies, dinner, bowling, and to throw coins into the fountain at the mall.

We talked about our life, our past and plans for the future. We made each other laugh constantly. We shared secrets and stayed together until one of us would finally have to call it a night. First thing in the morning I'd be pounding on his door to pick up where we left off.

A totally awesome spouse makes time to play. They know that recreation, laughter, and making new memories are essential in keeping their relationship in tip top shape. It's the active ingredient in building friendship between two companions and keeping that friendship alive and strong. A totally awesome spouse doesn't stop dating when they say "I Do". They let nothing stand between them and their friendship building moments with their spouse.

There are excuses that every couple uses from time to time. But no excuse is valid. If we want to become a totally awesome spouse, we must continue to regularly schedule time for dates.

The standard excuse: "We can't afford to go out." I've learned that we can't afford not to. Divorce is a whole lot more expensive and not nearly as much fun. As tight as money and time gets, if spending time one on one with our spouse is a priority, we will make it happen. To combat the "we can't afford it" myth and to get the wheels turning, I'm including a list of cheap and memorable dating ideas at the end of the book. My favorite is number three!

Totally awesome spouses play. They make certain there is time set apart for fun and laughter; free of children, distraction, and demands.

A Totally Awesome Spouse
Creates Common Ground

"I devote time, thought, and energy into creating common ground where my companion and I stand together, forever united."

There are several different types of personality tests. Through the years I've taken basically all of them. I've gotten a good outlook on who I am, along with my strengths and weaknesses. When Brock takes a personality test we can bet on one thing; whatever his results are, mine will be quite different. On one particular occasion there was a synopsis of the different personality types outlining which ones are compatible and which ones are not very compatible. Brock and I were on the *highly* incompatible list and it gave several reasons why these two personality types would struggle if blended.

Everything it said was true. It reflected many of the stressors that we deal with on a regular basis, just trying to live together day to day. I'm someone who likes to be right and who has an inner need for control and constant productivity. Brock avoids confrontation at all costs and loves to chill. I love to save money; Brock can't keep it in his pocket. I enjoy playing sports; Brock enjoys watching sports. I love Chinese food; Brock would rather eat dirt. Brock loves Blues; I love Christian rock. The list could fill this entire book. But you get the picture. Not only are many of our likes and dislikes on opposite ends of the spectrum, but a few of our core personality traits seem quite contradictory.

A totally awesome spouse appreciates everything about their companion. They see differences as just that, differences. They don't see them as character flaws, reasons to criticize, or something inherently awful. They choose to love their companion because of these differences, not in spite of them.

It's been quite a growing experience being married to a man who is so different than I am. But one day he helped me come to a whole new level of understanding. I was crying and griping about some particular issue and he said, "Melody, do you want to be married to yourself? Would you be happier if God just made a replica of you and zapped me out of the picture?"

That stopped me in my tracks. If I had to be married to myself it would be a complete and total disaster. I can imagine the magnitude of my pride, my need to be right, my control issues, my sensory issues, and my complete avoidance of spending money going head to head with someone with the same issues- it would be awful!

Looking back, I can see how our differences have brought balance. Of course things would've been easier here and there if we were even slightly more similar, but I know it was in His wisdom that God brought us together. We have learned to make our relationship work, how to appreciate what each of us brings to the table, and how to recognize the positive aspects we each contribute.

Differences are good and help balance our marriage. But it's also vital to have some common ground. A totally awesome spouse devotes time, thought, and energy into creating that common ground. They don't simply hope for it; they help it happen.

A totally awesome spouse is willing to do things their companion wants to do. They go to sporting events, concerts, and restaurants they wouldn't otherwise choose. They attend theater, craft shows, and social gatherings that may not have been on their high priority list. They make a conscious effort to learn to enjoy the things their spouse enjoys. And even when the activity doesn't jive with them on any level, they simply enjoy the time with their spouse and recognize the happiness they bring their spouse by choosing to be there with them.

A totally awesome spouse is creative in their strategies to create common ground. They read books together, find classes to take together, try new movie genres and attend a variety of events neither of them have ever tried . They may take up gardening, woodwork or pottery. They may start collecting something or redecorating. Memories are made and alliances strengthened. Sometimes they discover new things that they both instantly love. Other days they walk away united in their distaste for the new activity or laugh together as they mark it up as a waste of time.

A totally awesome spouse appreciates differences and they find ways to create common ground regardless of those differences.

By embracing all that is good in our companion, we are able to create an environment that allows us to grow and develop together. Through each effort our lives and passions are brought closer together and become entwined in a way that keeps us intimately united. Rather than moving further apart through the years, we will become more and more connected.

A Totally Awesome Spouse

Chooses Happiness NOW

"I am a happy and positive person. I choose happiness now and forever."

Too often we are waiting to be happy. We think that the next raise, promotion, or new job will bring happiness. We think that if we were just a bit thinner, more successful, or our hair was a new shade we'd be happy. If our spouse would do this or do that, then happiness would come for sure. If we won the lottery happiness would be ours forever.

But happiness isn't dependent upon anything external. Happiness comes from within. It's a decision. And it's personally attained. No one else can create or destroy our happiness.

Brock read a book a while back titled "Man's Search for Meaning" by Viktor Frankl. It was about a man who spent many years as a prisoner in a concentration camp. This man watched men and women all around him become bitter and full of hate. Love gave way to anger; hope was replaced by despair. He saw their spirits break and their will to live diminish. He watched as darkness filled their body and soul. He saw their hearts literally fail and their mortal lives end.

This man determined to never allow the soldiers to break him; to not let his heart fail. He realized that no matter what they did to him and how intensely horrifying conditions were, they did not have power over one thing. They had absolutely no power over his attitude. They could hurt, starve, and beat him. They could force him to perform intense labor and in the most dire of environments, but they could not force him to change his attitude. They could not force him to choose sadness above happiness, despair above hope, or hate above love.

That exercise of agency was his only freedom. It's a freedom that each one of us holds; no matter our circumstances, gender, age, financial status, physical condition, or how we are treated. We determine our attitude. We are in control of our happiness.

A totally awesome spouse chooses to be happy and they choose to be so *now*. They don't set requirements or expectations before they let happiness come. They take responsibility for their attitude. They know that their attitude determines their altitude and they choose to soar above the clouds. If you've read my other books you'll notice a pattern; no matter what part of our life we're striving to develop awesomeness in, attitude is a key ingredient to success. Choose to be happy. Choose to be positive. And do it today! As we look for silver linings, God will bless us to see beautiful rainbows in the midst of every storm.

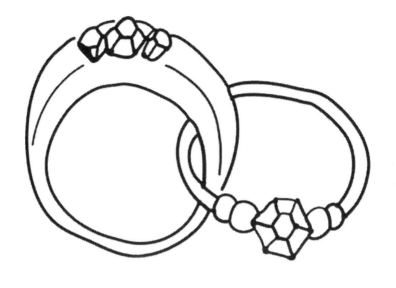

A Totally Awesome Spouse
is Faithful

"I am a person of integrity. Each thought I have, word I speak, and action I take is in harmony with the promises I have made. My faithfulness radiates light to my companion and to the world."

We live in a world full of deceit. We see corruption at all levels of society and government. We see marriages destroyed through lies and unfaithfulness. We watch as children suffer and hearts are broken. We see pain. We see fear. We see dishonesty.

A totally awesome spouse radiates light in this world of darkness. Their willingness to devote their heart and soul to one person shows incredible courage and faith. It is this courageous faithfulness that affords their marriage the best possible chance of survival.

Faithfulness is a decision. It's a decision to allow no one and no thing to take precedence over our spouse. It's a decision to place them in the forefront of our mind and keep them there at all times. It's a decision to consider the effect each thought we have, word we speak, and action we take will have upon them and upon our relationship.

"We divorced because he was unfaithful." We've heard this statement or a variant of it and our immediate thought was: "He had an affair." And very likely he did. But it's imperative to understand that faithfulness includes much more than just keeping other people out of our bed.

Through the years both Brock and I, at different times, have placed people, schooling, jobs, and things ahead of one another. As I look back, my vision is 20/20. When I was solely focused on school, our relationship suffered. When he was exclusively occupied with developing knowledge and skill in photography, our relationship suffered. When I placed all my time and energy into a management position and later when he devoted his passion to succeeding in sales, our relationship suffered. When I made a girlfriend into my best friend and when he preferred hanging with the guys to hanging out with me, our relationship suffered. I'm sure you can see the pattern.

Don't misunderstand; a woman needs girl time and a man has need for time with the guys. These needs are important and deserve to be met. Personal aspirations are important as well. The point is simply that they don't belong as the highest priority.

Faithfulness is placing our marriage as our highest priority. A totally awesome spouse places their companion ahead of friends, work, community service, personal ambitions, recreation, other family, and even their children. We change jobs, friends come and go, children grow up, and the world always needs volunteers. If our highest priority remains our spouse through everything that comes and as the years pass, we will create a relationship that is stronger than anything we will face and an incredible level of friendship, that sadly, too few marriages ever experience.

If the thought of putting your spouse ahead of your children sends you into a panic, stop to contemplate the broken homes and sadness that come from marriages that end. When a husband and wife love one another, when their relationship is strong, when they are devoted 100% to keeping a flame burning between them, the children are blessed with stability and security. The family stays together and enjoys feelings of unity and love.

There's an object lesson I'd like you to try. You'll need a mason jar, a bag of rice, and five golf balls. Place the balls in the jar and fill it to the very top with rice. Notice how the rice falls in nicely around it and fills in all the gaps. Now empty it all into a bowl and try do it in reverse. When you put the rice in first and then try to fit in the golf balls, there isn't room. A fair amount of the rice will spill out or you may not be able to fit the balls in at all. If we keep this lesson in mind throughout our life, our marriage will be blessed. If our golf balls (our main priorities) are in place first, everything else we need to accomplish will find it's place. But if we put everything else first, we will fail at those things that really matter. A totally awesome spouse writes in permanent marker upon one of the balls, "My husband" or "My wife" and places it in the jar with care.

Our home, community, country, and world are blessed by spouses who put each other first, by spouses who are physically, mentally, verbally, and emotionally faithful.

A Totally Awesome Spouse
Prays- and then Prays some more

"I allow God to direct my path and to fill my heart with light and love."

Prayer is absolutely essential. A totally awesome spouse never goes a day without a conversation with God. Marriage can be amazing, wonderful, and totally awesome on so many levels. It's also really hard work. Even if you're married to the most wonderful person on earth there's going to be struggles and hard times.

Spouses who choose to keep God out of their marriage are putting themselves at a serious disadvantage. God wants to be a part of our marriage. He desires for our marriage to not only survive, but for us to find complete joy, satisfaction, and peace with our companion; to feel the love for one another that only He can give us.

No matter our religion, background, or current level of spirituality, if we turn to God seeking answers and help, He will hear us. No matter what we've done wrong, what mistakes we've made, and how dark our life has become, He will forgive us, lift us, and help us to find happiness again. No matter if our faith is great or small, if we will exercise that faith enough to kneel before our God, He will bless and guide us.

Brock and I had been married a few years when I fell into a very dark time. I don't have the words to adequately describe it, but I felt broken and clouded with despair. I felt incapable and unworthy. I felt removed from God and alone, unsure if I'd ever again feel His light.

In sorrow one evening I curled up in a ball and began to sob. My heart cried to my God but my lips did not move. Without intention, I bumped the CD player and it began playing a song titled "Only One" written by Emily Freeman.

The words of the song were heard by my ears but they were sewn into my heart by God's own hand. It was a woman singing of being broken, of being in darkness, and holding the shattered pieces of her heart. It was a song about me. The song climaxed with *"Only One can take the pieces of my heart and make them whole. Only One can part the darkness and bring light into my aching soul. . . What I cannot restore, He can."* It was then that I felt God hold me, that He helped me understand that no matter how broken I become, He has power to heal me and make me whole. And not only that He *can*, but that He *wants* to and He *will.* And He does so for each person who is willing to ask.

A totally awesome spouse takes responsibility to develop a personal relationship with God. Their spiritual development and growth gets a place in their jar, and not as a grain of rice. They write "God" on one of their golf balls and place it beside "Spouse". As we place God in the top of our priority list we will come to understand and develop God-like qualities. A totally awesome spouse who continues to develop their relationship with God is granted more love, peace, and understanding toward their companion. They develop compassion, empathy, patience, wisdom, and a forgiving heart.

When hard times come and questions arise, a totally awesome spouse has a solid and reliable friend to turn to for advice; a friend with all wisdom, understanding, and love.

A Totally Awesome Spouse
Has an Attitude of Gratitude

"I recognize each blessing that enters my life. I extend sincere appreciation at every opportunity and have an attitude of gratitude."

Gratitude creates total awesomeness. Every emotion we feel and thought we have sends out an energetic vibration to the world. Gratitude is the highest vibration. It attracts the most positive energy and radiant light that can be found in the universe. When we choose to recognize our blessings and express gratitude at every opportunity, our life is bound for greatness. We lift those around us and bring light into once dark places.

A totally awesome spouse appreciates everything good in their companion. They don't take for granted that their spouse will always be there; rather, they celebrate that they have someone beside them and offer regular heartfelt thanks. They choose to watch for and acknowledge every act of service, kind word, and effort made; no matter how big or small.

When I praise Brock for doing the dishes and say "Thank you!" he smiles and makes an effort to do them more often. But if he does the dishes and instead of a thank you he gets: "Dude, you forgot the seven pots and pans on the stove top and didn't wipe off the table!" he's not going to have much desire to attempt the chore next time. When I get up at 4:50 AM to make my hubby a lunch and instead of a thank you when he arrives home from work I get: "I sure did hate to see Peanut Butter and Jelly today." it makes me want to sleep in and have him go hungry for a week.

When we feel entitled and ungrateful, we shatter the potential for good feelings and positive growth. A totally awesome spouse takes advantage of every opportunity to offer appreciation and thanks. They choose to emit an energetic vibration that lifts others rather than tears them down. They are grateful for every blessing and good thing in their life and consequently create a happier and brighter existence.

A Totally Awesome Spouse
Expresses Love

"I express love frequently and in a variety of ways. I jump at the chance to say 'I love you' and strive to show my companion that my words are true."

A totally awesome spouse expresses love at every opportunity and in a variety of ways. They say it *and* they show it. One without the other often leaves a companion feeling empty and unsure. Love expressed via a variety of methods will create the strongest bonds and best fulfill the emotional needs of a spouse.

Saying "I love you!" is one way to express love. A totally awesome spouse whispers it, shouts it, writes it, and speaks it frequently and intentionally. My husband is a pro at this. For those of us who aren't, let's practice!

Service is another way to express love. When we strive to be aware of our companion and to help meet their day to day needs we show that we care about them. We show that we are aware of what's important to them and what they may be struggling with, that we're here to support them. When we serve them, help them, go beyond what's expected, and show awareness of their struggles, love is felt and bonds are strengthened.

Giving thoughtful and unexpected gifts is another important way to express love. When we were first married Brock would buy me things in an effort to show me he was thinking of me. I would panic about the money he was spending and the act of love would consequently be lost to me. He would misunderstand my reaction as a rejection of his love offering. Part of successfully expressing love is understanding the thoughts and concerns as well as preferences of our companion. Now he knows that I do love thoughtful gifts but that for me, a single daisy he picks with his own hand will bring more heart twitters than a dozen store bought roses.

Physical touch, both gentle and passionate, are wonderful expressions of love. Each of these deserve their own chapter so I won't expound upon them here.

We want to hear it, feel it, and see it. So does our spouse. Expressions of love that are heard but unseen, are not as powerful. Expressions of love that are seen but are unheard, are not enough.

Popular literature suggests that there is a style of expression that we each prefer and most attune to. I agree with that. But I also believe that a couple experiences the fullest joy and strongest love connection when a combination of all varieties are utilized. A totally awesome spouse puts the most effort into their companion's favorite love expression but they keep the others warmed up and on the bench. No player goes too long without getting a turn in the game.

*A Totally Awesome Spouse Knows
the Small Stuff Counts*

"I take advantage of each opportunity that has potential to brighten my companion's day."

If a husband desires to really turn on his wife and bring her to a state of ecstasy, he ought to try doing the laundry and taking out the trash. If a wife desires to become the object of her husband's fantasy, she could simply put on a football jersey and play catch out on a muddy field. Now of course those are scenarios based upon stereotype, but you get the idea. It's the small stuff that counts. It's the little things we do that actually make us irresistible and help us become the one person our companion would never want to live without.

A totally awesome spouse performs random acts of kindness. They write notes and leave them in sporadic places and at unexpected times. They do a few additional house chores so there is extra time to cuddle that night. They buy a treat and leave it on their spouse's favorite "chill" chair. They might sing a love song on their spouse's voicemail or place a brand new pen in their office drawer. They could sneak to their spouse's work and decorate their car with lipstick kisses on the windows and a bag of Hershey's kisses spread across the hood. They may fix things that are broken or make an effort to keep a particular area of the house clean or add an extra fluffy pillow to their companion's side of the bed. They might help the kids get their homework done before dinner so that evening the family could devote time to playing instead.

There's a million little things we can do every day. As we choose to be aware and become willing to act, we will begin to recognize what we can do to bring a bit of sunshine to our spouse's day. We can show them they are important to us by devoting just a minute here and there to giving them an extra reason to smile.

A Totally Awesome Spouse
Yields the Power of Touch

"I enjoy touching and being touched by my companion. I make time for non-sexual touch each day."

A hundred years ago nearly 99% of infants in orphanages died before they were seven months old. What a travesty. It took years for people to realize the significance of these deaths and how to correct the problem. They died because they were not touched. They were not held, caressed, rubbed, or patted. They had no physical connection with another human being and despite their adequate clothing, bedding, food, and medicines, their little bodies could not survive.

Just as with these precious infants; when there is no touch, marriages will die. We have an innate need to physically connect with other human beings. Within a marriage, this contact between husband and wife is vital. This need for touch is distinct and separate from our need for passion and sex.

Typically, a man's need for sex is greater and a woman's need for non-sexual touch is greater. However; both men and women have *both* needs and with effort and gentle communication a couple can successfully discuss and incorporate a plan that will meet each need.

Brock and I have discussed this principle quite a bit. Sometimes he'll hold me and jokingly say "I'm holding you just to hold you. I have no intention of even thinking about making love to you so don't you even dare try to go and get all turned on." When we can discuss our needs and even laugh together rather than get offended by them, marriage is a whole lot more fun.

A totally awesome spouse touches their companion at every opportunity. Gentle and light touches when passing by, holding hands when walking side by side, feet connecting or legs entwined when lying in bed, an arm around their waist or shoulders when proximity allows; the list goes on. Each spouse has favorite ways to be touched; it's important to learn them. Brock knows that rubbing my feet or massaging my back will bring me incredible joy. But for him, I need to pull his hair and gently scratch his skin to bring that same level of happiness and connection. When we discover and utilize our companion's preferred methods of touch, our "touch time" becomes a lot more powerful in creating bonds and uniting our hearts.

A totally awesome spouse consciously creates opportunity for non-sexual touch and by doing so continually brings new life and light to a marriage, life and light that is vital to its survival.

A Totally Awesome Spouse Collaborates

"I face obstacles with confidence and creativity, solving problems and addressing differences in a way that leaves both of us with a smile."

Spouses in a typical marriage compromise. They give things up to keep the other happy; but in reality, compromise often leads to both parties ending up sad or feeling gypped. Totally awesome spouses do something better than compromise, they *collaborate*! They combine ideas, needs, thoughts, and desires to create a plan that gets both partners what's important to them. They join forces and work together for the good of the team.

Brock loves to eat chicken. He'd eat it five times a day if he could; in fact, sometimes he does. The rest of us occasionally get tired of it but I feel it's important that we eat meals together as a family. We collaborated a great plan. I keep a supply of chicken in the freezer; cooked and ready to warm up and eat. If I've made taco soup for dinner but Brock's inner voice is begging for a fresh supply of white meat, in 1 minute and 30 seconds he can have it and we can still sit together as a family for dinner.

Not every problem we face will have as easy a solution as pre-cooking a chicken dinner. But a totally awesome spouse brings creativity and ingenuity to the table no matter what the issue. They collaborate with their companion to construct the best possible plan.

Occasionally we must sacrifice things that we want in order to gain what we want most. Sacrifice plays an important role at times within a marriage. It can lead partners to appreciate one another and to value what they gain through their willingness to give up something less valuable for something of more worth. However, in many instances, partners who are willing to collaborate ideas and add a bit of creativity will be able to solve problems and address differences in a way that leaves each spouse with a smile and a full plate of food.

A Totally Awesome Spouse
Kicks Anger to the Curb

"I respond with patience and grace, even when facing offense, frustration, and stress."

Every human being appreciates being treated with respect. No one actually enjoys being screamed at, torn down, ragged on, griped about, criticized, threatened, gossiped about, or treated as inferior on any level. There are a variety of things we do that literally kill our relationships. Every positive effort we make can be wiped right out of the picture by engaging in these deadly habits.

When I was growing up I never once heard my mother say something negative about my father; or vice versa. I'm sure they had their disagreements and hard times, but they didn't argue in front of us and they didn't scream at and bash one another. In fact I never witnessed anything other than loving support. My husband treats me in that way. He doesn't criticize me or tear me down. I remember one day when I really lost my temper and flipped out at one of the kids, dishing to them way more than they deserved. Feeling horrible about it I sat down and expected him to ask me what in the world my problem was. What he actually said was, "It's hard sometimes isn't it?" Rather than pointing out how far short I'd fallen from the mark in that moment, he offered me empathy and then held me with care. I felt understood, supported, and ready to do better in the future. If he'd responded with "What in the world is your problem?" I likely would've thrown up a line of defensive thoughts and spoken ugly words, separating myself from him and feeling even more alone and out of control.

A totally awesome spouse speaks words that create feelings of love and support. They are gentle. They are kind. They never condemn or criticize; instead, they empathize and then encourage.

Anger, and the actions that accompany anger, hold no place in the heart or behavior of a totally awesome spouse. They are free of this vicious and destructive emotion. It takes effort and time, but with constant dedication, prayer, and practice, we can be free of it as well. Anger brings darkness. It brings pain and regret. It takes away our agency and turns us into beings of instinct. Lives are lost, friendships destroyed, and hearts broken when this dark emotion takes control.

I had a friend once tell me that he and his wife loved getting angry and duking it out, screaming until they were exhausted and letting it all loose. They are now divorced.

A totally awesome spouse lets go of anger and pride. They release the negative behaviors, emotions, and habits exemplified by the world and glamorized in the media. They instead work toward and embrace feelings and habits that express concern, thoughtfulness, admiration, friendship, gentleness, loyalty, and love.

A Totally Awesome Spouse
is a Professional Mouth Manager

"My words bring light and love to all who hear."

A totally awesome spouse knows when to open their mouth and when to keep it closed.

Conversation is an essential part of marriage and the way we choose to go about it can make or break our relationship.

When their mouth wants to criticize and condemn, when it wants to express anger and dissatisfaction, or complain and speak harshly, a totally awesome spouse keeps it shut. Even if they have to pull out the duct tape or bite their tongue until it bleeds, they do not open their mouth and release these weapons of mass destruction. They are in control and they do not allow their mouth to take the reins.

When their mouth desires to offer words of praise, love, admiration, satisfaction, gratitude, and comfort, a totally awesome spouse opens it wide and clear.

Communication is noted to be one of the leading causes of divorce. I'd venture to say that the problem isn't actually being unable to talk. Most of us can open our mouths and make sound. We speak to various people and they are able to hear us and understand our meaning.

So what's the real communication issue? I believe there are two behaviors within marriage that are to blame for communication struggles. The first is created by a spouse who communicates with unkindness. And the second by a spouse who is unwilling to share their true thoughts or feelings.

In a typical marriage a spouse may develop habits of using sarcasm, retorting, abusive and cruel name calling, and using putdowns. They may make fun of comments or suggestions and belittle their companion's beliefs and ideas. Such a reaction to attempts at conversation cause a spouse to throw up a barricade. No one desires to be treated unkindly and a warning light goes off inside both their conscious and subconscious mind: "Conversation with this person is unsafe and causes pain." After a few painful experiences, intimate conversation naturally becomes less and less frequent; eventually nonexistent. When a person feels unsafe to express themselves, love cannot grow and the flame that was once lit between them will go out.

The second behavior is when a spouse is unwilling to share their thoughts or feelings. Our experience from a few nights ago may resonate with you on some level. Brock asked me if I wanted to watch a movie. I really didn't. In my mind I was thinking "Seriously, is that the only thing you ever want to do? Wouldn't you rather rub my feet or read me a book or play cards or have an awesome make out session?" But aloud all I said was "Sure." He could tell I wasn't very enthusiastic so he asked again, "You sure? We could do something else if you'd rather." And my response, "No, it's fine." He turned on a movie and I sat there annoyed and didn't cuddle with him. That night after prayer we each went to our separate sides of the bed to sleep alone.

Why do we do that? Why do we keep silent when our mind is racing with thought? We don't express our thoughts and then we punish our spouse for not knowing them! Perhaps we think we have some valid excuse, "Oh I just want him to be happy" or "If I speak up he's going to shoot me down anyway" or "His needs are more important than mine" or the worst "He knows but just doesn't care." These types of thoughts are often irrational and are always counterproductive to effective communication. If our spouse asks us a question we should answer it, and answer it truthfully.

While I sat there feeling sorry for myself I realized that I was doing a really terrible job of being an awesome spouse that night. I decided that the next time such an occasion arose I would just tell him. The very next night he asked again "Wanna watch a movie?" And I said "You know, Love, I'd really enjoy it if you'd read me a chapter from our book tonight." He responded "That sounds good. I'd like that." We cuddled and he read. Then we made love. It was a much better night for both of us than the night before and all it took was honestly sharing my thoughts with an attitude of respect and gentleness.

A totally awesome spouse manages their mouth well. When they speak, words of kindness and words of gentle truth are shared. Their willingness to remain temperate, even during times of disagreement, allows feelings of respect and peace to radiate during the conversation. They create an environment which allows for intimate conversation and feelings of safety. When their companion speaks in anger and unleashes weapons of mass destruction, a totally awesome spouse disarms those weapons by retaliating with only gentle words of love.

A Totally Awesome Spouse
Continues Personal Development

"I am worthy of love and care; my needs are important. I am unique and have much to offer the world."

I love the title Mrs. Litton. I am happy to respond to it. I feel good knowing I bear my husband's name. But my identity is not in one title. My identity is more than wife; it's more than mother, friend, daughter, EMT, teacher, neighbor, or author- I am more. I am a child of God. I am unique and I am of infinite worth. I am a combination of all my titles, abilities, personality traits, physical makeup, passions, dreams, knowledge, experiences, talents, skills, quirks, weaknesses, and strengths. I am Melody Boyer Litton. I matter. And so do you.

A totally awesome spouse becomes one with their companion. They learn to become united in purpose and to care for their companion as they would their own body and soul. This unity creates a beautiful and unbreakable bond between their two lives.

What a totally awesome spouse does *not* do is lose their own identity in the process. It's easy to lose ourselves in our titles, relationships, and responsibilities. It's easy to forget who we are and what we need when we are actively caring for a spouse, children, job, and others. But a totally awesome spouse knows that they are worth taking care of, that their needs matter, and that they are unique and valuable individuals with much to offer and much to gain.

My first car was a 1981 Mercedes SEL, born the same year I was. She was old but beautiful. She and I went everywhere together and had amazing adventures.

When I took a job in Alaska she came with me. She braved the weather, Canadian customs, and the Alaska Highway. She took me past beautiful scenery, Northern Lights, and a variety of animals including wolves and bears. She let me haul my friends and gear all over the state that summer. I fueled her up but did little else to care for her; I just trusted she would be alright and knew that every time I got in to turn the key she'd be ready to take me where I wanted to go; I was ignorant to her other needs. She never let me down and gave me all she had.

At the end of the summer, I was anxious to get home. A friend and I decided we were going to make it without stopping. And aside from changing one flat tire, we never shut off her engine. We drove three thousand one hundred miles in 56 hours straight. Mercedes, although worn out and exhausted, didn't complain. She just kept going. She got us home safely. But she never started up again. Her existence as my constant and reliable companion was over. There was no reviving her; her light was gone.

Mercedes was a diligent companion. She gave me everything and took no thought to care for herself. She never expressed her needs to me and I remained in ignorance to those needs. Perhaps she would've loved to have a bath, a tune-up, an oil change, a few new parts, and a nicely scented air freshener hanging from her rearview mirror. It's likely that a bit more rest and some tender loving care would've prolonged her life. Our relationship may have never come to such a tragic end. If only she had told me...

Obviously Mercedes couldn't tell me what she needed. Sadly, she couldn't actually talk. But we can. We can communicate our needs to our companion. We can tell him/her that we need a bath, a tune-up, and some new parts. We can share our goals and dreams and what it's going to take to keep us fresh and ready to continue on our journey. It wasn't my lack of love that led me to failing my totally awesome car; it was ignorance. A vehicle owner ought to consult his maintenance guide and a mechanic. Unfortunately, a spouse doesn't come with a maintenance guide. We can't expect our husband or wife to know what we need and how to give it to us unless we contemplate on it, figure it out, and then tell them. Mercedes also didn't have the ability to take care of her own needs. But we do. We can take the initiative and ensure our needs are met, pamper ourselves, and continue personal development. By doing so, we can keep our light from going out; our mind, heart, body, energy, and soul in tip top shape.

A totally awesome spouse knows they are worth taking care of, that they are unique individuals with much to offer the world. They allow themselves to have personal dreams and goals, to pamper themselves on occasion, and to continue lifelong growth and personal development. When we are at our best, we can give our best to others. A totally awesome spouse drops a ball into their jar titled "Me". It does not represent selfishness. It represents their individual worth, their need to be taken care of, and their willingness to take action to address their needs.

A Totally Awesome Spouse
Overcomes Addictions

*"I maintain perfect self-control and personal integrity.
I am free of addiction."*

Addictions deprive us of our freedom. They often steal our health and rob our bank account. They destroy self-control, self-respect, and personal agency. They negatively affect our relationships and influence nearly every aspect of our lives. We become slaves to addiction long before we realize it.

I've attended addiction recovery classes at various times throughout my life. Sometimes because I'm curious about what they teach and the benefits I can gain for my own life and at other times I've gone to support friends or family. The first time I ever attended one I wasn't sure what to expect. I pictured walking in and seeing a bunch of unkempt, rough looking men with dirty clothes and un-brushed hair. But that wasn't at all what happened. The class was put on by a local Christian church and was designed for individuals with any type of addiction; to help them recognize, find hope, and take action to overcome their weaknesses with the help of Christ. Rather than a group of scary creepers walking in the door, I witnessed a variety of clean, respectable, and educated individuals enter the room. I recognized local church leaders, teachers, parents, and friends.

As the meeting progressed I took note of the different issues that each person dealt with. There was an incredible variety of addictions including drugs, cigarettes, alcohol, pornography, eating disorders, sugar, wasting money, perfectionism, caffeine, OCD, sexual issues, gambling, gaming, internet usage, shopping, and hoarding. Some addictions seemed minor to me and others severe. But as I sat there I saw pain in their eyes along with guilt and shame. I came to a realization that night; the devil doesn't really care what our addictions are. He just cares that we have them. Every addiction, whether large or small, begins inching us away from light and into darkness. It takes away our power to create the life we want and distracts us from what matters most. It begins to diminish our self-respect and often inhibits our physical, mental, and spiritual self from being at our highest potential. It takes from us our freedom to act and compels us to do as it demands.

A totally awesome spouse regularly pauses to do a personal inventory. They are courageously honest with themselves and open to acknowledging their flaws, mistakes, and any addictions that are trying to steal their personal power and separate them from the ones they love. Once acknowledged, they take every step necessary to take back their control and re-enter the light. No matter how trivial, how large, or how small the addiction may be, they take note of it and come up with a plan to conquer it. They recruit the help and aid of their companion and seek professional help when needed. No addiction is a safe addiction and every addiction deserves to be conquered.

I've seen marriage after marriage destroyed by unaddressed addiction; let's take action now to ensure ours is not the next.

A Totally Awesome Spouse
Keeps Secrets

"I am worthy to hold the confidences my companion shares with me. I create an environment where my companion feels safe and understood."

To become a totally awesome spouse we've got to be perfectly honest. We must be trustworthy. Our companion needs to know that we are worthy to hold the confidences they share with us. It's imperative that they know we respect them enough to keep their secrets and that we trust them with ours.

Intimate conversation is essential to creating loving bonds and a fulfilling marriage. Alone with our spouse is when we ought to be able to share our deepest feelings, our most powerful fears, and to admit our weaknesses and failures. Our companion must be able to trust us with these things. They need to know that when secrets are shared with us they will be kept safe and not broadcast to friends or the world. Facebook has been the end of more than one marriage and a gathering of chatty women or boisterous men has been the cause of more than one betrayed and broken heart. Whenever public laughter is enjoyed at the expense of a companion, private tears will certainly be shed.

A totally awesome spouse keeps their companion's secrets but *they do not keep secrets from their companion.* If anyone approaches them about anything and the conversation begins or ends with "don't tell your husband/wife..." then the conversation needs to end. Aside from an occasional surprise party or unexpected gift, there is no safe or acceptable reason to keep a secret from a spouse.

If a companion was suddenly able to read the mind of their totally awesome spouse there would be no surprises. A totally awesome spouse shares their thoughts, feelings, emotions, preferences, needs, and desires with honesty and in an attitude of love. They earnestly listen when their companion chooses to do the same. They respect their companion enough to keep silent when entrusted with information not meant for the world to hear.

A Totally Awesome Spouse
Looks Good!

"I respect my body; it is deserving of love and care. I am healthy, clean, and appealing."

Appearance matters. Whether or not we want to admit it, how we look is important. Our spouse was likely initially attracted to us because of the way we look and how we cared for ourselves. When we let our appearance go down the drain we are putting ourselves, and our marriage, at a disadvantage.

A totally awesome spouse looks good. They take care of their physical appearance. They shower and brush their hair. They brush their teeth, wash their clothes, and wear clean socks. They shave and groom their nails. They pay attention to what goes into their mouth and ensure nutritional balance with the food pyramid as their guide. They exercise and keep their bodies fit.

A totally awesome spouse is rarely a super model, Olympic champion, or found under the title "America's sexiest person." But they make an effort to take care of themselves, to pay attention to the message their physical appearance is sending to their spouse and to the world. They are not obsessed with their weight or wearing only the latest fashions or being the media's version of beautiful, but they do respect themselves enough to care for their body and appearance.

I have a few outfits that Brock loves for me to wear. He finds me most attractive with long hair and with natural shades of makeup. I make an effort to accommodate those preferences.

I love biceps. I get giddy inside when I feel muscles bulging from my husband's arms. When he makes an effort to keep his arms in shape I feel all kinds of happy. He likes to shave his head but when he does I think he looks like a serial killer and it drops him twelve steps on the attractiveness scale in my head. He's come to realize that it's worth it to pay someone to cut his hair rather than just taking the clippers to it.

When we can do simple things to become even more appealing to and align with the preference of our spouse, why wouldn't we? We live in a world that has easy access to running water, soap, laundry machines, razors, makeup, healthy food and fitness equipment. Let's take advantage of these conveniences and keep ourselves looking good, smelling nice, and radiating respect to ourselves, our companion, and others.

A totally awesome spouse makes a concerted effort to look good. They are not self-absorbed or preoccupied with appearance but they honestly assess their physical body and regularly take effort to keep themselves as healthy and appealing as they can.

A Totally Awesome Spouse
Loves Making Love

"I love making love!"

Sex is the most powerful and bonding act that we can perform in this world. It can unite hearts, bodies, and souls in a way that nothing else can. It yields the power to create life and the power to join together two lives in unity and love.

It's no wonder that the devil works so hard to destroy, discredit, and distort this wonderful gift. When we come together as husband and wife with love and pure desire to please one another, sex leaves us fulfilled and united. When we come together with lust, deranged ideas, pornography playing in the background, and self-focused attitudes, sex leaves us feeling alone and devalued.

Making love is a high priority for a totally awesome spouse. They understand that this bonding power is essential to keeping the best connection between themselves and their companion. They value this time between husband and wife and revere it with an attitude of respect and enthusiasm.

While visiting with a marriage counselor one day he suggested that sex should be scheduled; that a couple would be benefited by having their love making sessions on the calendar and given priority over things that may come up. I admit I laughed at him. I commented that that was the least romantic thing I'd ever heard. I was certain that making love ought be spontaneous and only performed in a moment of passion. But I've changed my mind.

After laughing at the counselor, the thought stayed in my mind and kept nagging at me. Finally I asked Brock what he thought of us scheduling certain days for making love and mentioned "We could do more too when we feel like it but these would be our standard times." I'm not sure why I was hesitant to broach the subject with him; after all, my husband is a man. He was beyond thrilled at the idea and in no time our new plan was implemented.

I now stand behind the suggestion of that wise marriage counselor. Schedule it, make it a priority, take turns being in charge of planning the details and look forward to the bonding that will occur. Drop a ball in the jar for making love.

A totally awesome spouse recognizes and respects the power and beauty of making love. They appreciate it as a gift and offer it without expectation or requirement. They share their needs and desires with their companion and listen with gentleness and love when their companion shares their needs and desires as well.

A Totally Awesome Spouse
is a Team Player

"I am on the same team as my companion. We stand united and work together always."

If two spouses are playing on opposite teams, one of them is going to lose. Our goal as husband and wife must not be to win alone; but rather, to win each game standing side by side, hand in hand. Because in truth, if one of us wins at the expense of the other, we both fail at what matters most.

Life affords us opportunity after opportunity to be divided. It often attempts to place jobs, children, schooling, personal aspirations, political stands, ideas, goals, and demands between us. A totally awesome spouse plays for the team. They find a way to unite themselves with their spouse to conquer each situation which arises and barricade they face, to set goals and have dreams that bring them closer to one another rather than further apart.

A totally awesome spouse recognizes personal weaknesses and requests aid from their companion. They recognize limitations their companion may have and offer help when it's needed. They give 100% always. They play to the best of their ability and trust the team (their spouse and God) to fill in the gaps and to make up for when they fall short.

A totally awesome spouse stands united with their companion. They make plans, do chores, carry out responsibilities, and address their needs and the needs of their children in a way that ensures continual respect and unity.

Selfishness decreases as our love and desire to become an effective team with our spouse increases. As we strive to meet their needs and unite our hearts with theirs we will be blessed with love and peace. We will not lose our identity; instead, we will come to know ourselves better and to comprehend the power and strength that comes from being on a team rather than playing this game of life alone.

A Totally Awesome Spouse
is a Money Managing Master

"I am wise with our finances and choose to live within our means."

There are wealthy couples who are incredibly happy and have wonderful marriages. There are also wealthy couples who are incredibly unhappy and have marriages that fall apart. There are very poor couples who are madly in love and there are poor couples who end up divorced. Money is blamed regularly for marital failure. But money is just money; being wealthy or poor can't rightly take credit for happiness or unhappiness, marital bliss or divorce. How we choose to manage the money we do have is what needs to be addressed.

A totally awesome spouse is in control of their spending habits. They are aware of the amount of money coming in and they pay attention to the amount that is going out. They understand debt and why it's not a good thing. They think before they spend and they use their head for more than merely a hat stand. Intelligently managing finances helps to avoid much heartache and severe stress within a marriage.

There are a variety of agreements and arrangements between couples in regards to money; whether both will work or one will stay home with the children, whether or not they will have shared accounts or separate, how the bills will be divided and who will keep up with ensuring they are paid on time, who monitors the budget, and whose name will be on what accounts. They each have pros and cons and I'm not going to attempt to convince you that one way is better than another. But each totally awesome spouse takes time to discuss their finances and come up with a plan that both companions are at peace with. When money management is left to take care of itself, a marriage will certainly face very hard times.

There are two things that totally awesome spouses always do. First, they ensure that both companions are aware of where money is coming from and where it's going. They are each accountable for understanding the bottom line and keeping it balanced. And second, they devote a set amount of money that each spouse gets that they are not required to be accountable for; they get personal "play" money. The amount doesn't matter, it could be $2 or $2,000 depending on the couple's finances, but being granted a set amount that is purely our own to be spent according to our own free will and choice is liberating and helps to counteract the strain of meeting other financial demands.

Money matters. The way we think about, talk about, address, and manage our money can greatly strengthen our marriage, or it has potential to be a large part in its destruction. A totally awesome spouse is financially savvy. They are money smart and help their spouse to be so as well. They make decisions regarding money and budgets with their companion and are patient and gentle as each person practices living within their means.

A Totally Awesome Spouse
Expels Poison

"Forgiveness comes naturally to me. I feel only love and compassion for my companion and quickly forgive when occasions arise."

I saved this chapter for last because all of the ideas, principles, and suggestions offered in this book will be void unless we understand and implement this important concept: *Forgiveness*. Without forgiveness we will never create the joyful companionship and totally awesome marriage that we desire. Forgiveness is essential. It's the active ingredient in every successful and happy marriage. No one is married to a perfect person. No matter how badly we desire to be, we aren't and never will be without fault and without weakness. At least not in this life.

We all mess up. We hurt one another and do stupid things. If we hold onto these offenses they will accrue within us to a point where we can no longer contain them. The pain will destroy us from the inside out. Not only must we learn to forgive our spouse for their faults, but we must learn to forgive ourselves as well.

Forgiveness is possible and forgiveness is liberating. Forgiveness is not accepting incorrect behaviors; it's simply choosing to not let the behaviors affect us in a negative way. It's about choosing love over hate, light over darkness, mercy over revenge, and patience over rage. It's about continuing to love and accept the person; to see them and their worth separate from their incorrect actions.

When we are wronged, a bit of poison enters our system. We then have a choice. We get to keep the poison and allow it to slowly work its way to our heart or we get to expel it.

I've messed up a lot through the years. I've caused my husband a lot of pain. Sometimes I've done things that have hurt him unintentionally and other times out of spite. He'd have valid reason to cut the rope and set himself free. Brock has hurt me as well. His weaknesses, habits, words, and behaviors have cut me to the core a time or two. There have been moments for each of us where the only reason we've stayed together is because we promised God that we would. And how grateful I am that we did!

At times a spouse has turned so far to darkness that abuse and violence has overcome them. In these cases professional and spiritual counsel is most certainly needed. With wisdom received through counsel and prayer, a spouse will know what is right in this difficult situation.

But for most couples, darkness can be overcome with a willing heart and through the grace and wisdom of God. The answer to most marital stress is not divorce, but rather, it is repentance and forgiveness. A totally awesome spouse learns to seek forgiveness and learns to extend it. They apologize and strive to make right the wrongs they have done and they accept the apologies of their spouse. Through the mistakes Brock and I have made we've come to understand the role that forgiveness must play in our lives and in our marriage. If we had chosen to hold onto each drop of poison our marriage would most certainly be dead. We would be miserable and our family would suffer.

A totally awesome spouse understands that forgiveness is key to having a happy and successful marriage. They place a "Forgiveness" ball in their jar and make it an active and vital part of every day. They flush their system of anger, revenge, self-pity, spite, pride, and annoyance. They turn to God and plead to be given the antidote for the poison. This antidote is the only thing that has power to clear the poison from our blood. The antidote is love; pure and unconditional love, God's love. When we choose love and light over anger and darkness our lives and our marriages are blessed. A totally awesome spouse accepts this love into their heart and soul; it fills them with peace, wisdom, and grace. It's what keeps them on the path of total awesomeness.

Melody Litton

Choose to be a Totally Awesome Spouse.

As we fill our lives with light and love, we radiate awesomeness to the world and learn to soar above the clouds.

Although we cannot force our spouse to fly, we can entice them with the beauty of the skies.

Our marriage will be blessed through our efforts and a joy currently unknown will be found.

We will become better people, companions, lovers, and friends.

Let's begin this beautiful journey today and never stop walking together down this road of total awesomeness.

Positive Affirmations

"I evaluate myself with honesty and love. I make desired changes with grace and confidence."

" I share my hopes and dreams with my companion. We are united as we set goals and create our totally awesome life."

"I offer 100% of myself to my companion. Together we find peace, strength and balance, even when surrounded by a world of chaos."

"I choose to love my companion now and forever. Our love grows stronger with each new day."

"I thoroughly enjoy recreational time with my companion. I schedule opportunities for laughter and play; free from distraction and demands."

"I devote time, thought, and energy into creating common ground where my companion and I stand together, forever united."

"I am a happy and positive person. I choose happiness now and forever."

"I am a person of integrity. Each thought I have, word I speak, and action I take is in harmony with the promises I have made. My faithfulness radiates light to my companion and to the world."

"I allow God to direct my path and to fill my heart with light and love."

"I recognize each blessing that enters my life. I extend sincere appreciation at every opportunity and have an attitude of gratitude."

"I express love frequently and in a variety of ways. I jump at the chance to say 'I love you' and strive to show my companion that my words are true."

"I take advantage of each opportunity that has potential to brighten my companion's day."

"I enjoy touching and being touched by my companion. I make time for non-sexual touch each day."

"I face obstacles with confidence and creativity, solving problems and addressing differences in a way that leaves both of us with a smile."

"I respond with patience and grace, even when facing offense, frustration, and stress."

"My words bring light and love to all who hear."

"I am worthy of love and care; my needs are important. I am unique and have much to offer the world."

"I maintain perfect self-control and personal integrity. I am free of addiction."

"I am worthy to hold the confidences my companion shares with me. I create an environment where my companion feels safe and understood."

"I respect my body; it is deserving of love and care. I am healthy, clean, and appealing."

"I love making love!"

"I am on the same team as my companion. We stand united and work together always."

"I am wise with our finances and choose to live within our means."

"Forgiveness comes naturally to me. I feel only love and compassion for my companion and quickly forgive when occasions arise."

Creative Dating Ideas

*Go ice blocking *Dress in formal attire and eat at McDonald's *Blow up an inner tube and float down a river *Make cookies and deliver them to friends *Go for a bike ride and have a surprise lunch waiting at your destination *Take bread to the lake to feed the birds *Wear grubby clothes and have a mud fight *Play catch at night with a glow in the dark Frisbee *Check the paper for free concerts and events *Park on a hill and watch the sunset *Pick berries *Go on a scavenger hunt *Create a treasure hunt for your companion and when you get to the end enjoy the treasure of goodies together *Grab a flashlight on a wet night and catch nightcrawlers together *Go fishing with your freshly caught worms *Take a hike *Roast marshmallows *Play at the beach or splash in a lake *Take a class together *Work out together *Teach one another a new skill *Visit a museum *Get a book at a local library about constellations and then spend the evening under the stars *Go to the county courthouse and watch a trial *Roller blade around town or at a local skating rink *Explore a cave or new mountain trail *Go rock climbing *Build something together *Paint or do yard work for a neighbor *Dress up like Mr. and Mrs. Santa Claus and go to local playground *Have a picnic breakfast at a local park in pajamas *Donate blood together and then go out for ice cream *Play golf in the snow with colored balls *Have a cooking contest *Search a cemetery for the oldest grave and leave it flowers *Buy a horrendous outfit for one another at a second hand store and wear them around town *Rent a bicycle for two or a paddleboat *Go sledding and bring along a thermos of hot cocoa * Play a board game in a public building *Split up at the mall with a $5 limit and see who can purchase the coolest item *Go bird watching *BBQ at the park *Have a play dough sculpting contest *Read a book aloud *Take a moonlight canoe ride *Sit on the roof together and count shooting stars *Have a candlelight dinner of cheerios *Volunteer at a local children's hospital *Go caroling *Visit a retirement home and cheer up the residents *Go to the Zoo *Build a snow man *Rake a pile of leaves and jump in them *Host a game night with several couples *Play air hockey *Make boats and race them down a stream *Have a whipped cream fight in the back yard *Go to an amusement park *Go swimming *Draw pictures of one another *Play an active Wii Game *Make murals with sidewalk chalk *Learn about Geocaching *Go to a department store and play with the toys *Have a water fight or set up a slip and slide in the yard *Plan a movie marathon with unlimited snacks and yummy food *Fly a kite *Gather needed ingredients from random neighbors and then use them to make cookies *Run through the sprinklers at a public park *Build a sand castle *Set up a tent in the backyard and order Chinese takeout to eat by candlelight *Play with animals at a local shelter *Make a list together of all the future dates you'd love to enjoy!

Melody Litton is a happy and energetic woman. She recently celebrated eleven years of marriage to her favorite person in the world. She is the mother of four "totally insane yet awesome" children. She has a Bachelor of Science Degree from Southern Utah University where she studied Interpersonal Communication and Sociology. She is a Nationally Registered EMT. Melody also enjoys working with others in teaching stress relief techniques including energy medicine and visualization exercises.

Melody's goal in writing the *How to be Totally Awesome* series is to bring a little laughter and some positive changes into the world.

She sees our world as a great place and believes that with a little effort we can make it even better.

Note from the Author

*I hope this book brought you smiles and encouragement.
I pray that it will help as you strive to make positive
changes in your life and in your marriage.*

*I ask that you take a moment to give this book an online
review and I welcome your feedback via e-mail at
totallyawesomebooks@yahoo.com*

*You, and your companion, are in my thoughts and
prayers.*

With love,

Melody Litton

Made in the USA
Charleston, SC
10 March 2013